100

THINGS TO DO IN
LEXINGTON
BEFORE YOU
DIE

100

THINGS TO DO IN
LEXINGTON
BEFORE YOU
DIE

AUDRA MEIGHAN

REEDY PRESS

Copyright © 2020 by Reedy Press, LLC
Reedy Press
PO Box 5131
St. Louis, MO 63139, USA
www.reedypress.com

Library of Congress Control Number: 2019952602

ISBN: 9781681062464

Design by Jill Halpin

All photos provided by Hillary B. Cooper unless otherwise noted.

Printed in the United States of America
20 21 22 23 24   5 4 3 2 1

Please note that websites, phone numbers, addresses, and company names are subject to change or cancellation. We did our best to relay the most accurate information available, but due to circumstances beyond our control, please do not hold us liable for misinformation. When exploring new destinations, please do your homework before you go.

DEDICATION

To my Matt who gave me Lexington and the world.

CONTENTS

• •

Music and Entertainment

• •

• •

Culture and History

● ●

Shopping and Fashion

● ●

● ●

PREFACE

I just love Lexington. Growing up nearby, it was always such a treat to visit the "big city," and as an adult I've seen it grow and become better every year. The people are so friendly that it's not uncommon to discover transplants who moved here simply because they fell in love with Central Kentucky on vacation. Entrepreneurs fascinate me, and this town is filled with some of the most passionate and innovative: I love supporting their local businesses. After years of creating itineraries for friends, family, and visitors, I decided it was time to actually write the book on it!

Some people scoffed I'd be hard-pressed to find 100 things to do here, but paring down the list was easily the most challenging part of the entire process. (Stay tuned for *100 Places to Eat & Drink!*) I encourage you to visit each of these places, chat with the great people who operate them, and start your own list of 100 more things to do. Now, with a nod to songwriter Stephen Foster, please enjoy a trip through "*My* Old Kentucky Home."

• •

ACKNOWLEDGMENTS

Writing this book has been one of the best experiences of my life, and I owe it to the friendly folks of my hometown. Thank you, Jules, David, Hillary, Morgan, Tareena, Joven, Ladonna, and Matt (again) for your encouragement and love.

Thanks to my family for always supporting whatever crazy dream I had each week, especially Chris and Gina, who have been my lifelong cheerleaders, and my book mentor, Mary. And to my friend Phil: I hope this makes you proud.

FOOD AND DRINK

SAVOR EXPLOSIVELY GOOD ICE CREAM
AT CRANK & BOOM

Locally sourced and ethically operated, with flagship flavors like Bourbon & Honey and Kentucky Blackberry & Buttermilk, Crank & Boom has quickly become one of Lexington's sweetest household names. The original location in the Distillery District has event space and a photo vault complete with fun props on a floor above the main area where guests choose from treats like a donut sandwich with ice cream filling, a complex sundae that might include bacon sprinkles, or a prosecco float with raspberry sorbet. A visit to either location means even more than a treat for the taste buds because staff are always engaging, friendly, and downright hilarious. Some smart Crank & Boom fans have even been known to skip eating a burger with fries to make this their main course instead.

Distillery District
1210 Manchester St., Lexington, KY 40504

The Barn @ The Summit
119 Marion, Suite 150, Lexington, KY 40517

(859) 288-2176, crankandboom.com

BELLY UP TO THE BAR
AT CHEVY CHASE INN

Known as the oldest bar in Lexington, Chevy Chase Inn may be the town's favorite dive. The atmosphere is dark, and a stark white sign hangs behind the bar reading "No Politics in CCI." Sometimes there will even be a politician's sign hanging above it to further prove this place has personality. Beers are filled from the bottom using unique taps and glasses, but bartenders warn you not to finger your drink or you will end up with a wet lap. CCI doesn't have food, but it welcomes guests to bring in Cajun dishes from the restaurant next door, and it offers live music on a regular basis. One reviewer even recommended this cozy hole-in-the-wall as a great place for the hearing impaired to enjoy the vibrations made by musicians. Although located in one of the most chichi neighborhoods, this affordable watering hole delights pretty much everyone who visits.

833 Euclid Ave., Lexington, KY 40502
(859) 266-9422

TIP
Street parking is free after 5:00 p.m. on weekdays and all day on Saturdays and Sundays.

TRY A TAMALE SANDWICH
AT PANADERIA ARACELI'S

The bakery walls are lined with cases of sweet desserts, but give your dentist some peace of mind and try a savory tamale instead! Panaderia Araceli's has stacks of red cafeteria-style trays that patrons pile with delicious rolls before watching them transform into a sandwich like no other. After paying for the rolls at the bakery register, folks line up in front of the many turkey fryers filled with every type of tamale possible: from mild pollo verde to the spicy rib tamale (watch out for the bone!). The tamale lady puts a bag on her hand, grabs the roll, cuts into it, and then uses tongs to pull your tamale of choice. Adeptly she unwraps the corn husk with the tongs, shoves the cornmeal coated goodie into the bread, pulls the bag around the sandwich, and twists the top closed so the steam softens the roll. The experience is as fun as the tamale is delicious!

481 NW New Circle Rd., Lexington, KY 40511
(859) 294-8317

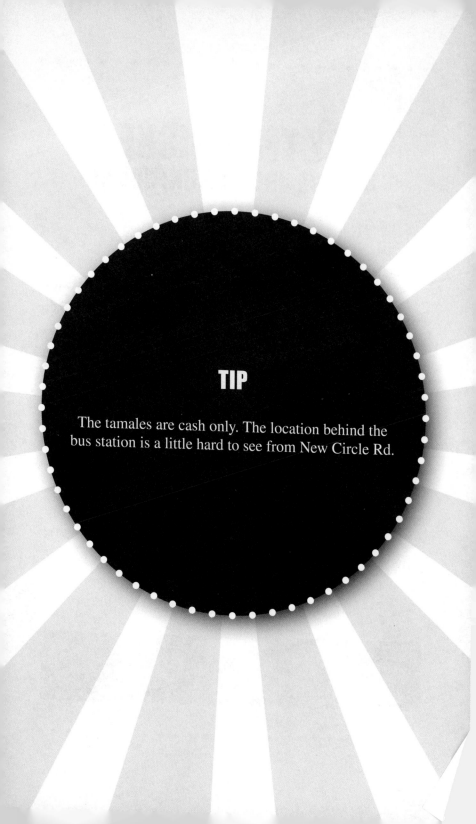

TIP

The tamales are cash only. The location behind the
bus station is a little hard to see from New Circle Rd.

TRY THE BRISKET
AT BLUE DOOR SMOKEHOUSE

The door is blue.

The seats are few.

It's the best place in town for good barbecue.

In the demographics of renowned barbecue, Western Kentucky is known for its mutton take, but in Lexington there is nothing like the brisket at Blue Door. It's a tiny place tucked into a neighborhood near the Warehouse Block entertainment district. You can smell the meat smoking as soon as you turn onto the street, and you're greeted with a line of friendly faces as soon as you enter. The meat plate is a great way to sample all the delicious offerings, which include traditional favorites like pulled pork and basics like sausage. After ordering, folks either wait for one of the few tables to become available or make new friends and share a four-top between couples. It's exactly the type of country charm and delicious food that makes perfect barbecue.

226 Walton Ave., Lexington, KY 40502

(859) 252-4227, bluedoorsmokehouse.com

TIP
If you want to try the brisket (and believe me, you DO), go early because they often run out.

DRINK AND DINE AL FRESCO
AT KENTUCKY NATIVE CAFÉ

"Oasis" is the best way to describe this little piece of paradise tucked behind one of the city's most renowned florists. There is no roof at this café. Sit outdoors amid some of the most beautifully curated organic foliage in the state. Craft enthusiasts can select from several local brews, and the bar includes wine and non-alcoholic drinks as well. Food selections are light, picnic-style choices such as a goat cheese and olive plate, quinoa salad, or Bavarian pretzels. Visitors meander with their refreshments through the trees as the leaves filter sunlight onto the walking paths. It's like a secret garden for those who want more than just the best patio in town.

417 E. Maxwell St., Unit B, Lexington, KY 40508
(859) 281-1718

TIP
The address is for the florist in front, but the parking lot is accessed via High Street.

DO-NUT MISS BREAKFAST
AT SPALDING'S BAKERY

Ask any Lexingtonian where to get the best donut, and one name is always mentioned: Spalding's. In 1929, Bowman and Zelma Spalding first created their infamously asymmetrical donuts by hand-forming dough to rise on birch boards before frying each circle to perfection. A visit to Spalding's Bakery is a step back in time: the building façade is an homage to the original location, family members draped in white aprons still greet you with a smile, and the old registers only accept cash just like nearly a century ago. Hungry people from all over the city line up before the doors even open to get their hands on a Spalding "original," otherwise known as the best glazed donut in town. Most locals stay true to the classic yeast glazed because of its reputation, but Spalding's is a full-service bakery that offers other donuts, cinnamon rolls, brownies, cakes, and cupcakes.

760 Winchester Rd., Lexington, KY 40505
(859) 252-3737, spaldingsbakery.com

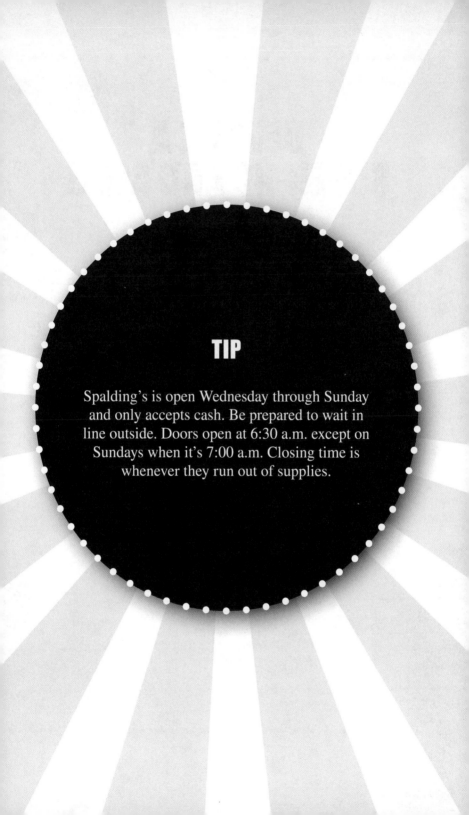

TIP

Spalding's is open Wednesday through Sunday and only accepts cash. Be prepared to wait in line outside. Doors open at 6:30 a.m. except on Sundays when it's 7:00 a.m. Closing time is whenever they run out of supplies.

DEVOUR A SUPER-HO AND ALE-8
AT TOLLY-HO

Lovingly referred to as "The Ho," Tolly-Ho is best known as the late-night nourishment spot for University of Kentucky students since 1971. It's everything you remember your favorite college diner being: dark, a little noisy, and satisfying. The Ho Burgers are juicy, and the fries are homemade. Locals skip the Coke or Pepsi argument here and instead enjoy the beverage made in nearby Winchester called Ale-8. It's most similar to a strong ginger ale and is completely non-alcoholic, even though its green bottle and vintage name often confuse out-of-towners. Everyone orders at the counter and there are arcade games to play while you anticipate the tasty food being lovingly prepared. Tolly-Ho is open twenty-four hours a day pretty much all year.

606 S. Broadway, Lexington, KY 40508
(859) 253-2007, tollyho.com

PLAN A DATE NIGHT
AT CARSON'S FOOD AND DRINK

With its crystal chandelier, barnwood walls, concrete floors, and library ladder back bar, you'd never know Carson's used to be a garage. It's Kentucky elegance at its best, and the food is as varied as it is delicious. Potentially the fanciest local restaurant in Lexington, it's the perfect place for a dressy night out and offers jazz on the patio and pre-prohibition style cocktails. Servers don suspenders and newsies hats and guide patrons through the extensive cuisine and bar menus. A suggested meal includes salmon bruschetta or the sausage trio; followed by the shaved prime rib or pesto chicken sandwich. To make it a true Kentucky experience, be sure to try Kern's Kitchen Derby Pie and a Woodford Old Fashioned.

362 E. Main St., Lexington, KY 40507
(859) 309-3039, carsonsfoodanddrink.com

TIP
Reservations are strongly recommended during peak hours on weekends and in the months of April and October when Keeneland is open.

SAMPLE
KENTUCKY WINE

The western states may have made Chardonnay a household name, but most people don't realize the first commercial winery in the country was established just outside of Lexington. While you might not find Cabernet Sauvignon, you will get to experience totally different varietals that thrive in Kentucky soil. The vineyards in Lexington are picturesque and a driving tour of them all makes for a lovely day. Talon Winery is known for being a go-to event venue and offers a Jazz on the Porch series where patrons can bring a picnic and enjoy tasting with a side of music. Grimes Mill Winery is a family-owned business that welcomes pets and offers two bocce ball courts for those who like activity with their tannins. Jean Farris Winery & Bistro lies along perhaps one of the most beautiful drives in town and has a gorgeous patio with high-end eats and a full bar.

Talon Winery
7086 Tates Creek Rd., Lexington, KY 40515
(859) 971-3214, talonwine.com

Grimes Mill Winery
6707 Grimes Mill Rd., Lexington, KY 40515
(859) 543-9691, grimesmillwinery.com

Jean Farris Winery & Bistro
6825 Old Richmond Rd., Lexington, KY 40515
(859) 263-9463, jeanfarris.com

TRY THE TAPAS
AT CORTO LIMA

Cleverly named for its location on the corner of Short and Limestone Streets, this Latin-inspired eatery is an anchor for the most popular downtown foodie district. The atmosphere is as bright and colorful as it is contemporary with a modern take on authentic cuisine. As one of Lexington's few true tapas bars, Corto Lima has a menu with something for everyone from vegans to carnivores. The blue corn emapanadas and steak rajas de poblano tacos are renowned, and there's always a fun new take on margaritas like mezcal or slush. The masa used for their tortillas is proudly ground on-site and every table gets different hot sauces to try. This intimate restaurant doesn't take reservations, so seating is limited for large parties, but it's always a great time and a treat for the tummy.

101 W. Short St., Lexington, KY 40507
(859) 317-8796, cortolima.com

TIP
Corto Lima is closed on Tuesdays. Street parking is free after 5:00 p.m. on weekdays and all day on Saturdays and Sundays.

HAVE DINNER FROM BEGINNING TO END
AT MIDDLE FORK KITCHEN BAR

Located in the burgeoning Distillery District, Middle Fork's rustic and cozy atmosphere is perfectly matched by the custom-built Argentinian wood-fire grill used to create what can best be described as food art. Every plate is masterfully arranged as a treat for the senses—visually beautiful, aromatic, and most importantly, rich and delicious. The menu is meant to be shared, and in true "tapas" style, dishes are served as soon as they are ready. Most of the meat is cooked over fire, and the eggs diavolo are a Lexington favorite. To complement the foodie experience, Middle Fork boasts a notable cocktail list arranged in an entertaining and informative manner. Perhaps a Suffering Bastard in Heaven will pair well with the Hog 'n' Oats.

Distillery District
1224 Manchester St., Lexington, KY 40504
(859) 309-9854, middleforkkb.com

TIP
The place is small, so reservations are highly recommended. Middle Fork is closed on Wednesdays and Sundays.

SAVOR SOUTHERN COOKING
AT WINCHELL'S

Despite sometimes being referred to as "Midwesterners," every Memaw and Papaw in Kentucky knows we're southerners when it comes to cuisine. There's no better place in Lexington to experience true home cooking than Winchell's. Located on Southland Drive in one of Lexington's coolest shopping and dining districts, Winchell's is a place where the servers learn your name and will greet you with "the usual"? A mix of greasy spoon diner and sports bar, Winchell's is big enough for large parties, but hospitable enough that you know you belong here. The menu includes breakfast favorites like trout and eggs and jalapeño cheese grits and Bluegrass specialties like beer cheese and Kentucky Hot Brown. And if you can't get tickets to a UK game, Winchell's is easily one of the most invigorating places to watch with other rabid fans.

348 Southland Dr., Lexington, KY 40503
(859) 278-9424, winchellsrestaurant.com

TIP
Winchell's also hosts special beer and bourbon dinners in addition to its annual lobster boil. Join their email list on the website or follow them on Facebook for details.

TAKE A TASTE-BUD TOUR
WITH BRUNCH IN THE BLUEGRASS

Lexington is a foodie town, and not in the cook-at-home kind of way—we like our haute cuisine served to us on a pretty patio with a side of Bluegrass hospitality and most certainly a cocktail. Since no self-respecting southerner would be caught dead imbibing before the clock hits double-digits, the rise of brunch was inevitable. Without a centralized source for all things related to the most important meal of the day, enthusiasts were forced to randomly search review sites and even (gasp) make phone calls until Brunch in the Bluegrass came to the rescue! Described as "a celebration of Central Kentucky's finest regional cuisine," Brunch in the Bluegrass is an incentivized, passport-style experience. They exist to help curate brunch selections, specials, and satisfaction through their active social media and blog, and participants can even eat and drink their way to free swag.

brunchinthebluegrass.com
facebook.com/brunchinthebluegrass
instagram.com/brunchinthebluegrass
info@brunchinthebluegrass.com

EXPERIENCE LOCAL
AT A OUITA RESTAURANT

Ouita Michel is arguably the chef in Lexington most recognized as bringing the farm-to-table movement to the Bluegrass. A perennial nominee for James Beard Foundation Awards, Ouita's restaurants include Honeywood, Zim's & The Thirsty Fox, Windy Corner Market and Restaurant, and Smithtown Seafood. Honeywood is a bright, big, and beautiful spot to enjoy a full-service meal and an extensive cocktail selection. Zim's & The Thirsty Fox are located downtown in the recently renovated Historic Lexington Courthouse and are perfect for a business lunch or after-hours cocktail. Windy Corner is located among horse farms and is fast-casual for sandwiches and the like coupled with gorgeous Kentucky countryside views. Smithtown Seafood is a fast-casual concept, with a location in the Jefferson Street dining district and at the Summit in South Lexington. Whichever style suits your needs, you're guaranteed a delicious experience.

TIP
Street parking is free after 5:00 p.m. on weekdays and all day on Saturdays and Sundays.

Honeywood
110 Summit at Fritz Farm #140, Lexington, KY 40517
(859) 469-8234, honeywoodrestaurant.com

Zim's & The Thirsty Fox
215 W. Main St., Suite 25, Lexington, KY 40507
(859) 785-3690, zimscafe.com

Windy Corner Market and Restaurant
4595 Bryan Station Rd., Lexington, KY 40516
(859) 294-9338, windycornermarket.com

Smithtown Seafood at West Sixth
501 W. Sixth St., Lexington, KY 40508
(859) 303-4100, smithtownseafood.com

Smithtown Seafood at The Summit
The Barn, 119 Marion St., #160, Lexington, KY 40517
(859) 309-0011, smithtownseafood.com

GRAB BREAKFAST
AT WHEELER PHARMACY

Wheeler's is the sole Lexington survivor from a time when your local pharmacy was also your soda fountain, convenience store, and diner. Visitors can grab a turquoise pleather–clad booth or spinny counter stool to peruse the menu while keeping an eye out for famous regulars like UK Coach Cal or Joe B. Hall, who frequent the place early. Renowned for their breakfast food and friendly service, Wheeler Pharmacy also offers a full lunch menu with specialty milkshakes and floats at fantastic prices. While the eggs are amazing, the Buddy Burger (double patties) for under $7 is also highly recommended. When it's time to check out, diners can either pay with cash at the counter or use a credit card at the pharmacy register.

336 Romany Rd., Lexington, KY 40502
(859) 266-1131, wheelerpharmacy.com

DRINK FAIR TRADE
AT THIRD STREET STUFF

Third Street Stuff has such a unique and funky style that Lexingtonians have been known to actually use its name as a verb like when explaining how they're going to refurbish a piece of furniture: "I'm going to Third Street Stuff it." Whimsically decorated inside and out, every surface is highlighted with signature purple, orange, green and black swirls, triangles, checkerboards, and inspirational quotes. Patrons sip on organic fair-trade coffee while tucked away at colorful tables or lounge on the comfy upholstered couch in the entry area. Lunch-goers can select from a full menu of locally sourced baked goods, salads, and sandwiches to enjoy inside or on the patio. Third Street Stuff is also well-known in the community for their support of various non-profits, Pride, and the LGBTQ community. It's easy to see why people come for the coffee and stay for the atmosphere.

257 N. Limestone #1, Lexington, KY 40507
(859) 255-5301, thirdststuff.com

SAMPLE SUSHI
AT TACHIBANA

You might think a land-locked state in a city with no natural waterways would never have fresh seafood, but then you'd be missing out on one of the best dining experiences in Central Kentucky. Lexington is a diverse place, and Tachibana takes pride in sourcing the freshest ingredients to create the most authentic Japanese cuisine in town. Oil-paper umbrellas and colorful flags dangle from the ceiling to cozy up the spacious area, which includes a sushi bar, Hibachi grills, authentic Tatami room (low tables on Tatami mats or flooring), and private Karaoke room. Don't be intimidated by its authenticity, though: the staff are extremely friendly, patient, and happy to help educate first timers. Tachibana is a destination eatery, but its proximity to the interstate and several hotels makes it a perfect spot for people on their way into or out of town.

785 Newtown Ct., Lexington, KY 40511
(859) 254-1911, tachibanarestaurant.com

TIP
Tachibana closes every day from 1:30 p.m.–5:30 p.m. and is always closed Sundays.

EAT LIKE A LOCAL
AT STELLA'S KENTUCKY DELI

Country crooner Barbara Mandrell used to sing, "I was country when country wasn't cool." Similarly, Stella's was Kentucky Proud long before local and farm-to-table became the buzzwords they are today. For decades, this colorful converted home has stood tall in the now-thriving Jefferson Street dining district serving breakfast and lunch goodies like the grilled PB&J, breakfast burrito, lentil burger, and Hot Brown sandwich, all made with the finest ingredients nearby farmers have to offer. It's a quaint and cozy restaurant where you may have to wait for a table, but you can spend your time perusing the bakery case for the day's display of desserts including whole pies. When the weather is nice, there are tables outside and the service is always friendly and helpful. Stella's also offers libations including wine, beer, cocktails, and a great selection of bourbon.

143 Jefferson St., Lexington, KY 40508
(859) 255-3354, stellaskentuckydeli.com

TIP
Street parking is free after 5:00 p.m. on weekdays and all day on Saturdays and Sundays.

PAY IT FORWARD
AT A CUP OF COMMONWEALTH

"1 Large Coffee for any volunteer"
"Any drink for someone who will sing a duet"
"Iced tea for a woman with the initials A.M."

These are just a few examples of the hundreds of cup sleeves pinned to the Pay It Forward board at A Cup of Commonwealth, where the motto is "Embrace community. Serve others. Create culture." You feel that mission in everything they do. The baristas are always friendly and welcoming, and often silly and entertaining both in person and on social media. They'll do everything from promote events and non-profits to just be downright funny for the sake of it. Oh yeah, and the coffee is delicious too! The roaster of choice is Magic Beans, and there's always a light and dark option along with pour-overs, French press, cold brew, and non-coffee drinks like tea and apple cider. In addition, there are baked goods and light food for sale along with cool logo swag. The place is so beloved the owner even had to open another location dedicated to all things cocoa. It is known as Chocolate Holler.

TIP
Street parking is free after 5:00 p.m. on weekdays and all day on Saturdays and Sundays.

A Cup of Commonwealth
105 Eastern Ave., Lexington, KY 40508
(859) 255-0270, acupofcommonwealth.com

Chocolate Holler
400 Old Vine St., Suite #104, Lexington, KY 40507
(859) 523-3619, chocolateholler.com

CHILL OUT
AT SORELLA GELATERIA

In the trendy NoLi (North Limestone) district, amid the array of "cool" old buildings, sits Sorella Gelateria—one of the only places to get authentic gelato in Lexington. Run by two delightful sisters, the atmosphere is bright and crisp with rotating art displays on the brilliant white walls. The day's selection of gelato usually includes a mix of traditional favorites like pistachio or chocolate and adventurous flavors like blackberry ganache or peach ginger lemonade sorbet. Locals follow their social pages to find out what's cooking for the day and clamor for their now-famous Biscoff and Nutella creations. All the gelato is made on-site with fresh and inspiring ingredients, so visitors will always have a fun variety to peruse.

219 N. Limestone, Lexington, KY 40507
(859) 797-0085, facebook.com/sorellagelateria

TIP
Sorella's is closed on Mondays and will alter hours seasonally. They update Facebook daily with this information. Street parking is free after 5:00 p.m. on weekdays and all day on Saturdays and Sundays.

DRIVE IN
TO THE PARKETTE

A classic drive-in diner, The Parkette has been a landmark in Lexington since the time it was reached only by dirt roads. Today, the place serves some of the same recipes the owner created when it opened in 1951, including some of the best fried chicken in town. The vintage pink and green neon sign beckons to locals and visitors alike to pull in and step back to a time when rock 'n' roll was king and food traveled to your window by roller skate. In addition to car-side service, hungry patrons can head inside for a *Happy Days* diner experience, complete with black and white checkerboard floors, plastic booths, and counter service on chrome and cherry-red stools. When there's no band playing, the retro jukebox has plenty of options to enjoy with a strawberry shake and a side of fries.

1230 E. New Circle Rd., Lexington, KY 40505
(859) 254-8723, theparkette.com

DIVE INTO
OLE HOOKERS BAIT & TACKLE
AND BAR & GRILL

This bar is such a dive that even Guy Fieri hasn't heard of it. With a tagline like "You're sure to catch something," Ole Hookers is not for the faint of heart. Run by one of Lexington's favorite entrepreneurs, this colorful place is her lifelong dream realized. It's dark, the walls are covered with local artwork and paraphernalia from funky events, and there is always someone hilarious ready to share a tall tale or unbelievable anecdote. True story! The pours are generous and the bar hosts entertaining theme nights like Hump Day Bingo, where winners can choose a prize from the "crap table," which is usually whatever was found on clearance that week. For those looking to make a lifelong memory in Lexington, Ole Hookers Bait & Tackle and Bar & Grill is just the place to do it.

203 S. Limestone, Lexington, KY 40508
(859) 317-9547, facebook.com/olehookers

TIP
Street parking is free after 5:00 p.m. on weekdays and all day on Saturdays and Sundays.

TACKLE THE BIG BREADSTICK
AT JOE BOLOGNA'S

Joe Bologna constructed a second floor between the stained-glass windows of this former synagogue to create enough seating for one of Lexington's favorite Italian eateries. The signature specialty is listed inconspicuously on the menu under the heading "Sides" as "one garlic breadstick." Closer in size to a small loaf of bread, it's served on a long tray of garlic butter, and tradition is to sprinkle (or dump) grated parmesan right into it before dipping. The adventurous and authentic will appreciate the sfincione pizza, which features anchovies, but traditionalists can still choose from classics like eggplant parmesan, stromboli, lasagna, and antipasto. Joe Bologna's offers beer and wine and sweet treats like gelato and cannoli for dessert.

120 W. Maxwell St., Lexington, KY 40508
(859) 252-4933, joebolognas.com

ORDER THE
FRIED CHICKEN
AT GRIMES'S FAST FOOD RESTAURANT

A certain colonel from southern Kentucky may have gained the chicken international fame, but when Lexingtonians get a hankering for finger-licking goodness, we head to Grimes's. Known as Richie's until its 2018 expansion into two locations, the Grimes family's restaurant has been hooking people on their unique recipe for thirty years. Service is walk-up or drive-through, and while the place is always hopping, the friendly employees welcome newbies and regulars alike to try their signature hot & spicy or regular fried chicken. The menu also includes fish, and while the potato wedges are their most popular side, they dish up pretty much all the southern classics, including candied yams, baked beans, and potato salad.

325 Roosevelt Blvd., Lexington, KY 40508
(859) 255-0445

4248 Saron Dr., Lexington, KY 40515
(859) 523-8222

grimessfastfood.com

FANCY A CUPPA
AT GREENTREE TEAROOM

Pip pip and cheerio to all those who fancy a spot o' tea! Greentree Tearoom is a lovely old home converted to a luncheon and event space with fine period furnishings, antiques, and vintage tea wares. Ladies and gents don their finest attire for a visit to this one-of-a-kind experience in historic downtown Lexington. White linen tablecloths laden with classic china, perfectly appointed cloth napkins, and fresh floral arrangements invite lunch-goers to sit and enjoy an ever-changing seasonal five-course experience. Teacups are refreshed regularly with the day's choice of Darjeeling, Nilgiri, or Assam, and piping hot scones are served fresh from the oven accompanied by homemade lemon curd and Fayette cream. The final two courses are available on a buffet, so every visitor gets their fill at teatime.

521 W. Short St., Lexington, KY 40507
(859) 455-9660, greentreetearoom.com

TIP
Reservations are required and seatings are at noon Wednesdays through Saturdays or by appointment. The menu is the same for everyone, so call ahead to discuss any special dietary restrictions.

TRACK LOCAL CRAFT
ON THE BREWGRASS TRAIL

What better way to experience all the delicious craft beers in Lexington than by following a trail that connects them and ends with free swag? The Brewgrass Trail extends throughout the state, but eleven of the breweries can be hit without ever leaving city limits. Passports are available at all participating beer vendors and VisitLex downtown. Participants merely need to ask for a stamp at a minimum of six locations before being eligible for a Brewgrass Trail t-shirt. More information about designated driver tours and events can be found at VisitLex.com, and lexbeerscene.com.

Blue Stallion Brewing
610 W. Third St., Lexington, KY 40508
(877) 928-2337, bluestallionbrewing.com

Country Boy Brewing
436 Chair Ave., Lexington, KY 40508
(859) 554-6200

Business Park, Lane's Run
101 Innovation Way, Georgetown, KY 40324
(502) 709-9943, countryboybrewing.com

Ethereal Brewing
Distillery District, 1224 Manchester St., Lexington, KY 40504
(859) 309-1254, etherealbrew.com

Fusion Brewing
Distillery District, 1170 Manchester St. #150, Lexington, KY 40508
(859) 554-8037, fusion-brewing.com

● ●

Lexington Brewing and Distilling Company
401 Cross St., Lexington, KY 40508
(859) 255-2337, lexingtonbrewingco.com

Mirror Twin Brewing
725 National Ave., Lexington, KY 40502
(859) 447-8146, mirrortwinbrewing.com

Pivot Brewing
1400 Delaware Ave., Lexington, KY 40505
(859) 285-6778, pivotbrewingcompany.com

Rock House Brewing
119 Luigart Ct., Lexington, KY 40508
(859) 368-7064, rockhousebrewing.com

West Sixth Brewing Company
Breadbox Original Location
501 W. Sixth St. #100, Lexington, KY 40508
(859) 705-0915

Greenroom, 109 W. Main St., Lexington, KY 40507,
(859) 705-0915

Farm, 4495 Shadrick Ferry Rd., Frankfort, KY 40601
(859) 705-0914, westsixth.com

Wise Bird Cider Co.
Distillery District, 1170 Manchester St., Ste 140
Lexington, KY 40508
(859) 309-1863, wisebirdcider.com

MUSIC AND ENTERTAINMENT

SKATE, SHOOT, AND SCORE
AT CHAMPS ENTERTAINMENT COMPLEX

One of the most exciting moments for every '80s kid in Lexington was getting an invite to a birthday party at Champs. Skating in the blacklight, dropping to the floor and kicking those heavy skates when the DJ yelled "GATOR," and spending five dollars of quarters in the claw machine to win a cheap stuffed unicorn was the best way to spend a Saturday afternoon. Since then, the local teen staple has expanded and become a complete entertainment destination for all ages. Visitors can choose from blacklight Mayan-themed mini-golf, tri-level laser tag, and arcade games. A new laser maze is a fun challenge, and there's a restaurant serving all the important favorites like nachos and pizza but also catering to parents with a full coffee bar.

297 Ruccio Way, Lexington, KY 40503
(859) 268-3888, visitchamps.com

HIT A HIGH NOTE
WITH LEXINGTON OPERA HOUSE

Lexington Opera House is nineteenth-century style at its best: red velvet drips from door frames, balcony entrances, and the proscenium arch. Ornate golden trim on every wall glistens from the gleam of the crystal chandeliers and wall sconces. You can almost feel the spirits of visitors past with their coattails and satin elbow gloves.

The seating area, intimate like the stage, holds fewer than one thousand attendees for some of the premier performances in the region. Lexington Opera House offers shows unlike any other in town, including nationally touring Broadway shows, ballet, opera, children's theatre, comedy, and bands. Located in one of the busiest entertainment districts in Lexington, this landmark is a perfect place to book for date night.

401 W. Short St., Lexington, KY 40507
(859) 233-4567, lexingtonoperahouse.com

TIP
Street parking is free after 5:00 p.m. on weekdays and all day on Saturdays and Sundays.

SPEND SOME QUARTERS
AT ARCADIUM FOR OLD DIMES SAKE

Part geeky childhood dream and part ironic speakeasy, Arcadium is the perfect place to satisfy every well-adjusted "Xillenial." Located in the trendy NoLi (North Limestone) district, this establishment is stocked with the best of old school arcade games, so you can battle Donkey Kong while enjoying a PBR or drink away your Galaga loss with a good Ol' Fashioned. The historic building sports exposed brick walls, original wood floors, and a private back patio that regularly hosts the finest and most unique Lexington food trucks. The bourbon and brew selection is vast and the bartenders knowledgeable and artful, so even if you aren't a gamer, the cocktail and craft experience is still well worth a visit.

574 N. Limestone, Lexington, KY 40508
(859) 317-9712, arcadiumbar.com

STARGAZE
AT THE LIVING ARTS & SCIENCE CENTER

In addition to being one of the most stunning and dichotomous examples of architecture in the city, The Living Arts & Science Center is Lexington's best-kept secret. The visionary center was established in the East End in the 1960s before STEAM was even a vision for most educators and parents. Based on the now commonly accepted belief that art and science intrinsically feed each other, LASC provides interactive programming to reach every demographic. The original historic Kinkead House underwent a massive addition in 2016 that more than doubled its footprint and added a Glo Gallery for artist exhibitions, computer lab, science hall, professional teaching kitchen, and Lexington's only planetarium. The grounds now boast a waterfall and stream system with native Kentucky plants, butterfly and children's gardens, an outdoor classroom, and local art pieces.

362 N. Martin Luther King Blvd., Lexington, KY 40508
(859) 252-5222, lasclex.org

GET THE BLUES
AT TEE DEE'S

Kentucky is known for its Bluegrass music, but Lexington knows Tee Dee Young for the blues. A Lexington native, Tee Dee's childhood biography reads like a screenplay where a young boy starts picking a guitar sitting on the railroad tracks, eventually finds a mentor in an older, seasoned musician, and ultimately performs in talent shows and basements and sneaks into clubs through back entrances for a chance at stage time. Tee Dee's unique blues style is upbeat and danceable and has earned him recognition from the blues capital of Memphis, Tennessee. A favorite way to get the blues is by visiting Tee Dee's bar on Second Street for open mic on Monday nights. The show doesn't start until at least ten o'clock, but with its diverse audience, cheap cover, and incredible music and atmosphere, it's well worth planning an afternoon disco nap and staying out late on a school night.

266 E. Second St., Lexington, KY 40507

TIP

The bar is only open on Monday nights,
but fans can follow Tee Dee online to find him
playing all over town.

DANCE THE NIGHT AWAY
AT THURSDAY NIGHT LIVE

Thursday Night Live started in 1995, and it could be argued that it has single-handedly created one of downtown Lexington's most hopping event venues. Hosting different musical acts every Thursday night from April through October, this revered concert series might be the most well-known and attended happening outside of Keeneland racing and University of Kentucky sporting events. In addition to music and dancing, attendees can expect food trucks, beer and wine tents, and lots of socializing with old neighbors and new friends. Hosted at Fifth Third Bank Pavilion, this event is always pet- and kid-friendly and happens rain or shine. Visitors are encouraged to truly make a night of it with dinner at any number of the hottest nearby restaurants and a stroll to a park, bar, or museum in the area.

Fifth Third Pavilion at Cheapside Park
251 W. Main St., Lexington, KY 40507
downtownlex.com/signature-events/central-bank-thursday-night-live

TIP
Street parking is free after 5:00 p.m. on weekdays and all day Saturday and Sunday.

CATCH A CONCERT
AT MANCHESTER MUSIC HALL

One of Lexington's favorite event venues in one of its most esteemed locations, Manchester Music Hall regularly hosts some of the region's best live music. The structure was originally built as the Old Tarr Distillery Warehouse #2 in the 1800s and served as bourbon barrel storage for the first part of its life. Now, after some much-needed structural upgrades, its Kentucky-style interior provides a beautiful and expansive place for people to party. Patrons can peruse the website to find which upcoming acts they'll enjoy most, and those who aren't certain can even take a "Find Out Your Music ID" quiz. No matter what event you decide to attend, you're sure to enjoy a good time with a full bar and plenty of choices.

899 Manchester St., Lexington, KY 40508
(859) 537-7321, manchestermusichall.com

ENJOY FINE MUSIC
WITH LEXINGTON PHILHARMONIC

Created in the 1960s for the purpose of providing background music to a University of Kentucky film, the original Lexington Philharmonic musicians were all volunteers. Since those humble beginnings, LexPhil has become a premier source of the arts in Central Kentucky. Every year, they hold over two hundred concerts and programs across the Commonwealth. Most often, the performances are at UK's Singletary Center for the Arts, but special events often occur at the Opera House and area churches as well. LexPhil hosts guest artists and is always innovating to make every patron's experience an exciting and fulfilling one. Before performances, they also partner with The Boone Center nearby to offer cocktail hours and dinner.

Offices, 161 N. Mill St., Lexington, KY 40507
(859) 233-4226

Regular Performances
Singletary Center for the Arts, 405 Rose St., Lexington, KY 40508
(859) 257-4929, lexphil.org

TIP
Street parking is free after 5:00 p.m. on weekdays and all day on Saturdays and Sundays.

HURL A HATCHET
AT BATTLE AXES

Let's face it: axes are cool. You don't have to be a lumberjack to throw an ax, but it is encouraged to wear your favorite flannel to Lexington's premier hatchet-throwing destination, Battle Axes. After signing a waiver, folks are guided to an area with wooden bullseyes and protective fencing where a "pit boss" teaches safety and the art of the throw. After leading some practice sessions, pit bosses become scorekeepers and referees so groups can start getting competitive. All this ax heaving can make a person thirsty, so Battle Axes offers over seventy beers and ciders in addition to soda, bottled water, and snacks. While the idea of hurling a sharp object over your head at a board a few feet away may seem intimidating to some, Battle Axes offers different style tools and techniques so even the most timid are on a level playing field.

Distillery District, 1170 Manchester St., Suite 160, Lexington, KY 40508
(859) 687-0069

401 Outlet Center Dr., Suite 350, Georgetown, KY 40324
(502) 642-4509, battleaxesky.com

LAUGH
AT COMEDY OFF BROADWAY

Consistently voted one of the country's top ten comedy clubs, Comedy Off Broadway is renowned for its national and international acts. The venue is intimate, so everyone feels like a VIP whether the night's performer is a stand-up comic, hypnotist, magician, ventriloquist, or even a shaky "open miker" just working out some new material. COB doesn't serve food, but there is a one-drink minimum and the club's motto is "It doesn't have to be alcohol, but we're a whole lot funnier if it is!" Tucked into a favorite Lexington shopping destination, Comedy Off Broadway's location makes it the perfect spot for date night so couples can browse the stores, grab dinner, and then take a seat for what promises to be the most entertaining show in town.

161 Lexington Green Cir. #C4, Lexington, KY 40503
(859) 271-5653, comedyoffbroadway.com

TIP
For aspiring comics, COB offers open mic nights regularly—check the website for details.

EXPERIENCE NEW ORLEANS
AT CREAUX

Cleverly named for a specific pronunciation and the New Orleans spelling of the word "Creole," this Short Street bar offers live music and a Louisiana-inspired menu. Crēaux (pronounced cree-oh) is the premier spot in Lexington for up-tempo jazz in a relaxed setting that's perfect for date night or an impromptu drink. The building is industrial with a façade of steel windows, worn wood floors, and exposed brick walls decorated with pop art. There's sidewalk seating perfect for people-watching and enjoying a drink like a Hurricane served in an Erlenmeyer flask. The music sets the mood for each night and ranges from quiet jazz on a Wednesday to upbeat horns and drums or serious dance music on the weekends. Crēaux is the best place in Lexington for a NOLA vibe and an always fantastic time.

310 W. Short St., Lexington, KY 40507
(859) 469-8960, creauxlex.com

TIP
Street parking is free after 5:00 p.m. on weekdays and all day on Saturdays and Sundays.

INDULGE IN NOSTALGIA
AT THE BURL AND THE BURL ARCADE

For those whose favorite way to spend a childhood Saturday was with a pocket full of quarters at a local arcade, and whose favorite way to spend an adult Saturday is with a refreshing beverage listening to great music, The Burl and Burl Arcade are for you. Located in Lexington's Distillery District, the two buildings share a parking lot and complement each other to create an entire evening of fun. The Burl hosts live music starting around eight o'clock, but The Burl Arcade opens much earlier, so many people will buy tickets to a Burl show and then pregame with some pinball and Super Nintendo next door. Both buildings are converted concrete block garages with some upgrades like polished concrete or hardwood flooring, a wall of retro TVs for gaming systems, and a rose window as a stage backdrop. If all that isn't enough, both locations offer full bars, there is a patio and a fire pit, and on weekends the place typically hosts a delicious food truck.

TIP
The Burl's age restrictions vary by show and the arcade does allow children at certain times. Call or email for details before you go.

The Burl
375 Thompson Rd., Lexington, KY 40508
(859) 447-8166

The Burl Arcade
369 Thompson Rd., Lexington, KY 40508

theburlky.com

STOP ADULTING
FOR A DAY
AT EXPLORIUM

Children's museums have grown exponentially in popularity and Lexington has the perfect example of why that's so. Located in The Square shopping center downtown, Explorium has several permanent exhibits that keep visitors coming back time and time again. One is Kids Court where little Bobby and Suzie can become judge, juror, or lawyer and play out an entire trial. Another includes an area specifically for toddlers called Wonder Woods that allows the smallest patrons to play with animals and insects and offers a playhouse with reading area. They also have rotating and visiting exhibits, and even offer a program where young artists can display and sell their work. Explorium achieves its mission of delivering fun in a "dynamic hands-on learning environment that inspires imagination and curiosity."

The Square
440 W. Short St., Lexington, KY 40507
(859) 258-3253, explorium.com

TIP
Street parking is free after 5:00 p.m. on weekdays and all day on Saturdays and Sundays.

HAVE A TIKI DRINK
AT GREEN LANTERN

For those who prefer their entertainment with a heaping helping of dive bar, Green Lantern is a perfect fit. Recognizable by its trademark colored patio roof, this quirky place offers interactions with any number of hilarious characters, including the bartenders, who will happily mix up a signature drink of their own imagination. There's a pool table on one side and a unique concept known as tiki java on the side with the stage. Tiki java is just that: rum cocktails and coffee drinks to keep patrons relaxed while simultaneously hopped up on caffeine. Located in the Jefferson Street Dining District, this cozy Lexington landmark keeps guests entertained with live music ranging "from doom metal to bluegrass, psychedelic to punk, and indie rock to folk."

497 W. Third St., Lexington, KY 40508
facebook.com/The-Green-Lantern-Bar-183595498351037/

SIP AND STROLL
AT LEXARTS HOP

Downtown Lexington organizations love their artwork and realize you don't have to be a certified museum or gallery to share creativity with the world. That's why LexArts Hop exists. Participants can not only visit actual galleries and studios, but also restaurants, gift shops, and even non-profits to mingle among incredible creations in interesting places. Admission is free at this event, which happens the third Friday of every other month, and exhibitors happily offer snacks, drinks, and lively conversation to visitors. LexArts is "greater Lexington's premier cultural development, advocacy and fundraising organization," and LexArts Hop encourages everyone to appreciate art on any budget. Interactive guides and maps are available online or physical brochures can be picked up at the LexArts downtown location on Mill Street.

LexArts Office
161 N. Mill St., Lexington, KY 40507
(859) 255-2951, galleryhoplex.com

WATCH A MOVIE
AT THE KENTUCKY THEATER

Prominently displayed on Main Street, the iconic triangular marquee lit with globe-shaped lightbulbs and pink neon outlining the all-capitalized name Kentucky beckons passers-by into a rich and ornate space to revisit a time when going to the movies was a special event. The Kentucky Theater has a long and tumultuous history, but today is Lexington's favorite destination for an indie movie or a vintage film on the big screen, and even the occasional live performance. In addition to enjoying the incredibly restored space and affordable ticket prices, show-goers can visit the concession stand for the usual popcorn and candy fare accompanied by a soft drink, beer, or wine. The Kentucky also offers first-run movies and different series, including the Wednesday Night Classic Movies and Midnight Movies.

214 E. Main St., Lexington, KY 40507
(859) 231-6997, kentuckytheater.com

TIP
Street parking is free after 5:00 p.m. on weekdays and all day on Saturdays and Sundays.

LISTEN TO LUDWIG
AT LEXINGTON CHAMBER ORCHESTRA

Lexington Chamber Orchestra's mission is "to call people into higher awareness and deeper community through the beauty of chamber music." Chamber orchestras are intentionally smaller than larger outfits like a philharmonic because the artists believe in a more intimate connection with the audience; imagine a Rolling Stones concert in a stadium versus an acoustic band at a local pub. Lexington Chamber Orchestra offers pay-what-you-can concerts to the community at well-known churches and iconic institutions like the Lyric Theatre. In addition to regular season shows, visitors who find themselves in the Bluegrass at summer's end can take in the Chamber Music Festival set in downtown. From Handel to Haydn and Chopin to Tchaikovsky, The Lexington Chamber Orchestra is a wonderful way to experience music in Central Kentucky.

lexingtonchamberorchestra.com

PLAY WITH THE KIDS
AT LEXINGTON CHILDREN'S THEATRE

Lexington takes its art very seriously, including our children's theatre, which is renowned for its local and touring productions. As one of the "oldest continuously operating theatres for young people in the country," LCT also holds the distinction of being the State Children's Theatre of Kentucky. Not only do they produce professional performances that appeal to all generations, they also offer sensory-friendly and pay-what-you-can shows.

If you're the parent to your own little superstar, he or she can take advantage of different acting classes and audition to be on stage in a production. Lexington Children's Theatre's location in the bustling Short Street entertainment district makes it the perfect spot for a day of family fun.

418 W. Short St., Lexington, KY 40507
(859) 254-4546, lctonstage.org

SPORTS AND RECREATION

STROLL
THROUGH THE ARBORETUM

Famous explorer Daniel Boone is quoted as saying "Heaven must be a Kentucky kind of place," and The Arboretum proves why. An idyllic setting to meander and meditate or ponder and pontificate, The Arboretum is a perfectly curated slice of the Bluegrass with a paved path through native plants and trees from across the state. In the fall, the trail is decorated with creative scarecrows designed by local students and families, and when spring rolls around those same spots are occupied by imaginative birdhouses. There's a children's garden where little ones can shovel, plant, and learn all about horticulture. The Arboretum is free and open daily, and they also host multiple events throughout the year, such as Lunch Hour Mindfulness Walks, plant exchanges, and gardening tutorials.

500 Alumni Dr., Lexington, KY 40503
(859) 257-6955, arboretum.ca.uky.edu

TIP
There is plenty of parking in the lot, but if UK has a home football game plan accordingly for heavy traffic.

ATTEND AN EVENT
AT RUPP ARENA

When people say "Rupp," Wildcat fans know they're talking about the home of our beloved University of Kentucky Men's Basketball team, but Rupp Arena has also been Lexington's biggest entertainment venue for over forty years. Built out of necessity to contain the rapidly expanding Big Blue fanbase, there is nothing like being surrounded by twenty thousand rabid devotees when it goes dark, the announcer's voice booms, and the spotlight settles on the tunnel from which some of the country's most elite athletes emerge. Visitors lucky enough to be in Lexington for a UK home game should definitely experience Big Blue Nation in all its glory, but if hoops aren't your thing, the venue also hosts concerts, professional wrestling, and family shows. The iconic Rupp Arena is located in the heart of downtown, so event goers can make a night of it with shopping, dining, drinking, and browsing.

430 W. Vine St., Lexington, KY 40507
(859) 233-4567, rupparena.com

LEARN TO PLAY PICKLEBALL
AT KIRKLEVINGTON PARK

Pickleball has been around since the '60s but is only recently gaining national notoriety. Its following in Lexington has grown so much that the city converted tennis courts at one local park into pickleball courts. Best described as a mix between ping pong and tennis, pickleball uses a solid paddle instead of strung racket and a wiffle-type ball that bounces. The best part about Lexington pickleball is that the game is so popular that a community of regular and committed devotees meet daily to play each other and educate newbies to the sport. Every morning in good weather, Kirklevington Park's courts are full of players rotating partners and competitors for several hours. When winter sets in, the group moves to a nearby church, and they're always welcoming to visitors.

396 Redding Rd., Lexington, KY 40517
(859) 288-2900, bluegrasssports.org/kpa/

TIP

The parking lot closest to the courts is located on Spangler Dr. Players show up as early as 8:30 a.m., but are usually gone by noon. Be ready to play and chat if you go—devotees love to teach newbies! Bring your own water, but experienced players will usually share equipment on your first time. Kirklevington Park has plenty of other amenities if you want to make a day of it or bring the kids.

VISIT WHERE IT ALL BEGAN
AT MCCONNELL SPRINGS

A drive to McConnell Springs can often be misleading, as every turn takes visitors past another industrial or commercial building, but the journey ends with a scenic and historic park to be explored. Before Kentucky was its own state, frontiers settled at this site, and upon learning about "the shot heard 'round the world" that began the American Revolution, named what would become our fair city "Lexington." It is aptly called McConnell Springs for its founder and its bubbling water features, accessible by a quick walk into the beautiful wooded grounds of the park. Hikers can enjoy an easy and well-established trail to discover remnants of all the structures that used to exist here, including a mill and distillery. In addition to its status as a recreational park, McConnell Springs takes pride in its educational outreach, including public tours and children's programs like the study of owl pellets.

416 Rebmann Ln., Lexington, KY 40504
(859) 225-4073, mcconnellsprings.org

PLAY DISC GOLF
AT VETERANS PARK

Veterans Park's disc golf course is one of the highest rated in Central Kentucky for its difficulty and beauty. Among the trees in and around the walking trail through the shady hillside, concrete tee boxes offer disc golf enthusiasts unique challenges for a full eighteen holes. There's a creek whose size varies with Lexington's rainfall, and loads of vegetation and massive trees with which to contend. The course is 5,151 feet long, with hole lengths all under 400 feet and more than half under 300. The holes may be short, but since most are in the woods players still feel challenged, and it gives them a perfect shady atmosphere on humid summer days.

After a rousing round, players can benefit from all the other park amenities, including art installations, fountains, picnic areas, a war memorial, and a playground.

650 Southpoint Dr., Lexington, KY 40515
pdga.com/course-contact?course=25675

BIKE, WALK, OR RUN
THE LEGACY TRAIL

The Legacy Trail takes pedestrians through Lexington's history with an appropriate beginning in the historic East End, the birthplace of local horse racing, and culmination at the Kentucky Horse Park, an education center dedicated to the state's most revered animal. Aptly named, the Legacy Trail is a refreshing way to witness the unique beauty the community works hard to conserve while also getting a taste of Bluegrass history. The paved trail is open to bikers and walkers and is dotted with community artwork, interpretive signage, and gorgeous views of Kentucky farmland. Boasting an uninterrupted twelve miles of trail, the Legacy is Central Kentucky's longest paved multi-use path and has challenging hills interspersed with moments of flat land. The Legacy Trail is perfect for staying in shape or for taking the family on a picnic hike.

TIP

For directions to the Coldstream Trailhead, use "Legacy Trail Parking Lot Coldstream" in your search. For directions to the Horse Park Trailhead, use Cane Run Baptist Church, 4526 Iron Works Pike, Lexington, KY 40511, as the parking lot is very close to it. The Northside YMCA has bikes and helmets available for rent.

Northside YMCA Trailhead
318 West Loudon Ave., Lexington, KY 40508

Coldstream Park Trailhead
McGrathiana Pkwy., Lexington, KY 40511

KY Horse Park Trailhead
Ironworks Pike, Lexington KY 40511

kentuckytourism.com/cycling-kentuckys-legacy-trail

SWING A CLUB
AT KEARNEY HILL GOLF LINKS

Many visitors are surprised to learn how affordable golf is in Lexington, and one of the most scenic courses to play a round is Kearney Hill. Influenced by the large Scottish population that settled in Central Kentucky, this course on the northwest edge of town has rolling green hills and sparse trees. The water hazards include three lakes, and there is a ten-acre practice facility. The gorgeous and large clubhouse features locker rooms, a pro shop, and a snack bar along with views of almost the entire course and several surrounding farms. Ranked one of the top ten courses in the state, it's often selected to host national tours and championship tournaments. Kearney Hill Golf Links is also recognized as a Certified Audubon Cooperative Sanctuary, meaning it is committed to preservation of its natural elements.

3403 Kearney Rd., Lexington, KY 40511
(859) 253-1981, lexingtonky.gov/kearney-hill-golf-links

TROT ON OVER
TO THE KENTUCKY HORSE PARK

Everybody knows the Bluegrass loves all things equine, and the Kentucky Horse Park is here to prove it. Dedicated to the relationship between human and horse, KHP is the only attraction of its kind in the world. Situated on more than 1,200 acres of rolling green hills, the list of attractions within is nearly endless but includes everything from museums and an art gallery to an educational theme park and horse-drawn tours. Special events happen annually, and the on-site campgrounds allow visitors to truly make a trip of it, never having to leave horsey-heaven even for a minute. For the finicky family member who's the only one without an appreciation for the ponies, there is also a multitude of other events: car shows, maker's markets, 5K races, book fairs, and holiday shows like the nationally recognized Southern Lights in December.

4089 Iron Works Pkwy., Lexington, KY 40511
(859) 233-4303, kyhorsepark.com

THROW BACK TO SIMPLER TIMES
WITH THE BLUEGRASS BARONS

Lexington is most well-known for its legendary basketball, but local lovers of America's pastime have brought baseball in its purest form to town. The Bluegrass Barons are Kentucky's only team in the Vintage Base Ball Association and play the game just as it would've been played in the 1860s. Waveland State Historic Site serves as an appropriate and beautiful backdrop to teams clad in pillbox-style caps and striped knee socks. A wooden bat cracks against a ball slightly larger than today's, and a bare-handed outfielder makes the catch as the umpire in a straw hat yells "Hand!" then turns to address spectators, explaining this means "out" in modern terms. Children witness the action with hot dogs in hand while seated on piles of hay bales and the wooden plank fence that borders the first baseline. Players take the game seriously, and most onlookers marvel at the lack of baseball gloves: catching the ball is often an audible experience.

Waveland State Historic Site
225 Waveland Museum Ln., Lexington, KY 40514
(859) 272-3611, facebook.com/Bluegrass-Barons-1630209400587347

TIP

Bring your own chair as seating is limited.
Concessions such as hot dogs, popcorn, and soft
drinks are available for sale.

SAY YOUR PRAYERS
AT LEXINGTON ICE CENTER MINI GOLF

Lexington is a diverse and inclusive community, and with Kentucky's location in the Bible Belt, it only makes sense that almost every local has played what is lovingly referred to as "Bible Golf." Lexington Ice Center's extremely unique theme for mini golf has earned it national media recognition, and it is a must-try for every visitor. With three outdoor courses, each set of eighteen holes has a biblical theme: Old Testament, New Testament, and Miracles, and it's a good idea to go ahead and play them all. Professional putters particularly will appreciate the ridiculously difficult challenge of getting a ball up the steep sides of Mount Sinai. Prayers might help to make par on Jonah and the Whale, which forces players to aim for what we'll politely call the "blowhole." After the game, there are concessions and ice skating available inside for anyone who wants to make a day of it.

560 Eureka Springs Dr., Lexington, KY 40517
(859) 269-5681, lexingtonicecenter.com

CHEER THE CHAMPION
LEXINGTON LEGENDS

Locals have been sporting fun fake moustaches since 2001, when Lexington Legends mascot Big L started using his hairy upper lip to root, root, root for our first-ever Minor League Baseball Team. Two-time consecutive South Atlantic League Champions, the Legends play games at Whitaker Bank Ballpark, home to bourbon and barbecue vendors as well as a gift shop for all things Legend-ary. A visit to the park is everything a kid could hope for: from hot dogs to popcorn, t-shirt cannon to kids' play area, a chance to catch a fly ball to the nightly closing fireworks, this place is designed for good family fun. Certain weeknights are themed, like twenty-five cent hot dog night and Thirsty Thursdays, and there are special events and nonprofit fundraiser nights like Bark in the Park as well.

Whitaker Bank Ballpark
207 Legends Ln., Lexington, KY 40505
(859) 422-7867, milb.com/lexington

TAILGATE
AT KEENELAND

Everyone anticipates spring and fall in the Bluegrass—and not just because of the seasons changing. April and October are Keeneland Racing time in Lexington! Ladies don their fanciest hats and gentlemen exchange their dark suits for peppy suspenders and pink bow ties to attend the most picturesque track in all of Kentucky. The rolling green landscape welcomes visitors and locals alike to tailgate at "The Hill" and watch the simulcast with new friends. General admission is only $5 for a chance to hobnob with the likes of national celebrities or the mayor. The magnificent horses parade around the tree-lined, iron-gated paddock before they line up on the track. Limestone walls guide the way to the viewing areas where patrons can place their bets, grab a bowl of hot burgoo, and sip a bourbon before cheering their pick to victory.

4201 Versailles Rd., Lexington, KY 40510
(859) 254-3412, keeneland.com

TIP

Navigating traffic as a first-timer can be difficult, since there are many different gates and areas, and locals refer to them all by different names. Be sure to plan ahead or go with someone who knows the parking layout. Also be prepared to wait in traffic when leaving. Keeneland is open year-round for simulcasts, betting, events, and dining.

TAKE A HIKE
AT RAVEN RUN NATURE SANCTUARY

Hikers, birdwatchers, and general nature lovers flock to Raven Run for its miles of trails and scenery within minutes of the city. Winding in and out of the shade on wooded hillsides bordering the Kentucky River, walking paths lead guests by wildlife, historic artifacts, and a vast array of native plants. In addition to stunning views, the park hosts a variety of events including yoga, Little Explorers education programs, stargazing with the Bluegrass Astronomy Club, guided fungi tours, wildflower viewing, and 10K and 5K trail runs as fundraisers. Experienced hikers will want to take the 4-mile loop to see it all, but there are several shorter options for those seeking a quick yet meaningful walk through Bluegrass woodlands.

3885 Raven Run Way, Lexington, KY 40515
(859) 272-6105, ravenrun.org

TIP
No pets allowed at this park, so leave Fido at home.

WITNESS A MIRACLE (LEAGUE, THAT IS)
AT BLUEGRASS MIRACLE LEAGUE

Since 2006, children and adults with disabilities have literally been on a level playing field because of the Toyota Bluegrass Miracle League. The field is located at Shillito Park, and there people of all abilities get to play baseball in a fun and rewarding environment. Everyone is a winner! It's as official as it gets, since there's even an announcer who knows the participants and keeps them and the spectators entertained. Visitors can enjoy an inspiring game and then anything else the park has to offer. There's a barrier-free picnic shelter nearby, and Shillito also has a pool, basketball and tennis courts, a playground, and plenty of walking trails.

Shillito Park
300 W. Reynolds Rd., Lexington, KY 40503
(859) 367-7515, bgml.org

TIP
Seasons are Spring and Fall only, so games are played in April, May, June, September, and October.

WITNESS REAL SKATING ACTION
AT ROLLER DERBY OF CENTRAL KENTUCKY

With names like Lady Smackbeth, Busty McFearsome, and Pinky Brewser, you know these ladies mean business. Roller Derby has come a long way from the choreographed and scripted shows most people remember, and the Roller Derby of Central Kentucky players are serious athletes. While the pageantry is as engaging as it is entertaining, ROCK bouts are a true display of skill, finesse, and brute strength. Blockers and jammers clad in helmets and pads skate around a flat track, pushing and shoving to score points while enthusiastic fans cheer on their favorite players. As with any unfamiliar sport, there are lots of rules to learn, but the players and their faithful followers are always eager to answer questions and spread the good news that is roller derby.

Lexington Convention Center
430 W. Vine St., Lexington, KY 40507
rollerderbyofcentralkentucky@gmail.com
rockandrollergirls.com

TIP

Spectators who want the fullest of experiences should opt to sit in "the danger zone," where the seats are close to the action.

PEDAL A BOAT
AT JACOBSON PARK

Every community has its specific "rites of passage," and to be a true Lexingtonian, that includes pedaling a boat on the Jacobson Park reservoir! Sunny summer days are the perfect time to take to the water and have some family fun. Visitors can choose from two- or four-person pedal boats or a two-person kayak if that's more your speed. Jacobson offers beautiful views of rolling green hills and lush foliage along with seasonal activities such as haunted trails in the fall and kite-flying in the spring. Take a break and take it all in while the dogs enjoy their own fenced area, the kids run around the playground, and the grandparents fish from the banks. The park also has a basketball and volleyball court in addition to plenty of picnic shelters.

4001 Athens Boonesboro Rd., Lexington, KY 40509
(859) 288-2900, lexingtonky.gov/jacobson-park

BALL AND BREW
AT MARIKKA'S

The local German restaurant doesn't usually conjure visions of sand volleyball—unless you live in Lexington, Kentucky. Marikka's started as a small place to get homemade wurst and schnitzel and to this day still has the best German eats in the city. Now in its third iteration, there are two sides to the building: the cozy restaurant and the giant sports bar boasting six sand volleyball courts. With three indoor courts, sports enthusiasts are able to play year-round, and the bar boasts a list of over a hundred beers for patrons to enjoy. There are nights with open play, but if volleyball isn't your thing, plan instead for dart boards, pool tables, air hockey, shuffleboard, or even just a great night of dining.

411 Southland Dr., Lexington, KY 40503
(859) 275-1925, marikkaslex.com

JUST DANCE

Lexington loves to dance, and there is a multitude of places you can get your groove on. From Latin to tribal and ballroom to belly, there is a place that caters to every style. In addition to the plethora of local studio options, there are also events like Swingin' on Short, where top area dancers teach enthusiastic newbies the Lindy Hop to upbeat jazz bands. The Salsa Center Dance Studio offers classes for its namesake spicy style. Mecca is the center for belly dance, flamenco, hula, African, samba, and hula hooping, and its stars can be seen at parades, including one where they perform the "Thriller" dance in October. The Ballroom House caters to couples with BYOB date night and the LGBTQ community with their Out to Dance offerings. Arabesque World Dance has yoga classes and performs belly dance around town for those who would rather appreciate from a distance than shake their own groove things.

The Salsa Center Dance Studio
817 Lane Allen Rd., Lexington, KY 40504
(859) 278-8598, thesalsacenter.com

Mecca
3270 Nicholasville Rd., Lexington, KY 40503
(859) 254-9790, meccadance.com

The Ballroom House
312 Southland Dr., Lexington, KY 40503
(859) 309-1362, theballroomhouse.com

Arabesque World Dance
451 Chair Ave., Lexington, KY 40508
(859) 455-8991, arabesquelex.com

BET ON THE PONIES
AT THE RED MILE

While the color most commonly appreciated in Lexington is blue, the local favorite for a different hue is the Red Mile. Another bucket list venue for lovers of Kentucky's favorite animal, the Red Mile is one of the oldest harness racing tracks in the world, and with its recent renovations, it's the top destination for gambling in the Bluegrass. Spectators can cheer on their picks outside and in between races head inside to grab a drink or snack, or fill the time with more betting at one of the many gaming terminals. The Red Mile is huge and in addition to gambling, food, and drinks, they offer live music, dancing, special events, and a rewards program for regular visitors to earn discounts and free stuff.

1200 Red Mile Rd., Lexington, KY 40504
(859) 255-0752, redmileky.com

CULTURE AND HISTORY

GET A HISTORY LESSON
AT VISIT LEX

Located in the beautifully restored Historic Lexington Courthouse, VisitLex is the first place everyone should see. New inductees to the area can email a postcard featuring the city mascot, Big Blue. There are learning kiosks all around the gorgeous space where people can get a quick lesson on anything from the weird and wild to the basketball and bluegrass. There's even a sniffing station to smell the differences in some of the most recognizable bourbons made in the area. To round out the incredible amount of information, there are also great mementos for sale like socks, glassware, clothing, and generally anything that's Kentucky blue, y'all.

Historic Lexington Courthouse
215 West Main St., Suite 75, Lexington, KY 40507
(800) 845-3959, visitlex.com

TIP
There are parking spots reserved on Upper Street, and the center validates for parking in the Short Street garage.

SIT A SPELL
AT WAVELAND STATE HISTORIC SITE

Nestled in one of the busiest parts of South Lexington, Waveland is a historic antebellum house with ties to famous explorer Daniel Boone, who is credited with discovering the "gateway to the West." Rumored to be haunted, the striking mansion is decorated with period-appropriate furniture, and tour guides clad in 1840s style dress tell the tales of plantation life in Kentucky. Historians regard Waveland as one of the Commonwealth's finest examples of Greek Revival architecture, with its lofty ceilings, columned front porch, and inset fireplaces. The grounds include several original buildings in addition to a barn for private parties, an herb garden, flower garden, and orchard. Waveland offers special events year-round, including Tuesday and holiday teas, ghost hunts, Victorian death customs presentations, and holiday events like Playtime with Mrs. Claus and a Dickens Christmas Carol.

225 Waveland Museum Ln., Lexington, KY 40514

(859) 272-3611, parks.ky.gov/parks/historicsites/waveland/

GET INTO THE SPIRIT
AT A LOCAL DISTILLERY

Aside from a rousing rendition of "My Old Kentucky Home," there is little that moves a Kentuckian to tears of pride like sharing the story of America's native spirit. It's well-known in the Commonwealth that there are more bourbon barrels in Kentucky than people. Lexington contributes to this statistic as home to four different distilleries, three of which produce bourbon and one which makes whiskey. What's the difference, you ask? Well, it's time for a distillery tour! Visitors will learn the legal mandates for bourbon in addition to the creative steps that make every brand taste so different. Stick your finger in sour mash, smell the "white dog" fresh from fermenting, and enjoy the process of what keeps Kentucky famous outside of livestock.

Barrel House Distilling Co.
Distillery District
1200 Manchester St., Lexington, KY 40504
(859) 259-0159, barrelhousedistillery.com

Bluegrass Distillers
Breadbox
501 W. Sixth St. #165, Lexington, KY 40508
(859) 253-4490, bluegrassdistillers.com

James E. Pepper Distillery
Distillery District
1228 Manchester St. #100, Lexington, KY 40504
(859) 309-3230, jamesepepper.com

Town Branch Distillery
401 Cross St., Lexington, KY 40508
(859) 255-2337
kentuckyale.com › products › town-branch-bourbon

TOUR
THE MONROE MOOSNICK MEDICAL AND SCIENCE MUSEUM

Only those most dedicated to knowing all things Lexington have even heard of this collection of weird, confounding, and downright odd nineteenth-century artifacts. Located within Lexington's Transylvania University, the collection was used to teach science and medicine in the early to mid-1800s. While at the time the items were considered cutting-edge technology, today's visitors often describe what they witness as more akin to science fiction than fact.

Bring a strong stomach to witness the medical curiosities of the day. One of the most infamous artifacts is a fourteen-inch diameter buffalo hairball which was believed to suck poison out of wounds when held against them. Marvel at the rare medical Venus, a wax human figure made with parts of nearly two hundred cadavers. There's no end to the surprises as new old items are regularly discovered among the boxes and shelves in storage as the museum has no permanent home.

300 N. Broadway Rd., Lexington, KY 40508
(859) 233-8300, jday@transy.edu
https://libguides.transy.edu/aboutspec/MoosnickMuseum

TIP

Tours are by appointment only and must be scheduled through Curator Jamie Day at jday@transy.edu. Best times are in March, April, October, and November. Donations are requested for tours.

FIND SOME
FIRST LADY INSIGHT
AT THE MARY TODD LINCOLN HOUSE

This impressive historic home overlooks Main Street in downtown Lexington and welcomes visitors with intriguing stories of Mary Todd Lincoln and the era in which she lived. From the home's sordid and haunted history to a look into the fascinating and creepy world of Victorian hair art, the Mary Todd Lincoln House is packed with authentic furnishings, and tours are led by extremely knowledgeable storytellers. Feel the hardwood floors creak beneath your feet as you investigate all fourteen rooms in this over two-hundred-year-old home. Listen to the story of our sixteenth president (who visited here in November 1847) through the lens of his Lexington-born wife. While the outbuildings no longer survive on the grounds, the Todd's large garden has been partially restored and offers visitors a relaxing and thoughtful respite after the tour.

578 W. Main St., Lexington, KY 40507
(859) 233-9999, www.mtlhouse.org

BROWSE ART IN THE PARK
AT THE LOUDOUN HOUSE

Loudoun House is often more appropriately referred to as Castlewood for the name of the park in which it resides and because it resembles a much more royal structure than just a house. The architecture itself, with its diamond-paned windows and multiple towers, is an art study all on its own, but upon entering you'll be greeted with an even greater feast for the eyes. Lexington Art League curates multiple exhibitions throughout the year, including watercolor, mixed media, prints, and handmade paper. Sculptures dot the building's grounds as well. After exploring the building and its contents, visitors can enjoy the vast park with its playground, butterfly garden, pool, tennis, walking trail, baseball field, basketball court, and picnic shelters.

209 Castlewood Dr., Lexington, KY 40505
(859) 254-7024, nps.gov/nr/travel/lexington/lou.htm

PAY RESPECTS
AT LEXINGTON CEMETERY

Lexington Cemetery is well-known for its parklike atmosphere, which includes exquisite architectural elements along with a full arboretum, nationally reputed gardens, and several lakes. Visitors are greeted by a stone arch and gatehouse before meandering through acres of historic graves, majestic trees, and lovely flora. As a final resting place the cemetery is as serene as anyone could hope, but it also offers a backdrop perfect for walkers, photographers, birdwatchers, and anyone who just needs some time to meditate in an idyllic setting. Tourists can visit the burial sites of any number of famous Kentuckians, including statesman Henry Clay and actor/comedian Jim Varney. Civil War buffs will find both Union and Confederate soldiers buried here as well.

833 West Main St., Lexington, KY 40508
(859) 255-5522 , lexcem.org

TOUR LEXINGTON HISTORY
AT HOPEMONT, THE HUNT-MORGAN HOUSE

Civil War buffs and general history enthusiasts will love touring the Hunt-Morgan House. A walk to the Federal-style home leads through downtown's lovely antebellum Gratz Park, and upon arrival the first thing visitors will notice is the impressive façade: the beautiful front doors are flanked by leaded side lights and an elliptical fanlight above. On the second story, an intricate Palladian window adds even more to the aesthetic. Upon entry, the foyer's vast and winding staircase is a sight to behold and the original wood floors glisten in the sunlight. A tour through all twenty rooms of the home is only enhanced by a stroll through the period garden, complete with brick walkway, wrought iron fence, flowering trees, shrubs, and a gazebo.

201 N. Mill St., Lexington, KY 40508
(859) 253-0362 , bluegrasstrust.org/hopemont

TIP
There is a small admission fee and the home is open from March through mid-December. Tours are offered on the hour from 1:00 to 4:00 on Wednesday, Thursday, Friday, and Sunday afternoons. Saturday's first tour is at 10:00 a.m. and its last is at 3:00 p.m.

EXPERIENCE TRIPLE CROWN VIEWS
ON A HORSE FARM TOUR

Kentuckians love our horses, and there is nothing more quintessentially Bluegrass than witnessing the breathtaking farms that house them. A horse farm tour is a chance to truly take in the scenery: white plank fences surrounding rolling green hills where majestic mares nuzzle their newborn foals in the late afternoon sun. Historic barns litter the hillsides and upon closer inspection are much fancier than just some outbuilding for a pet—they are palaces for equine royalty. Visitors can choose from group, private, or self-guided tours as Lexington offers a variety of ways to get up close and personal with the reason we are the "Horse Capital of the World."

TIP
Reservations are required, and peak times include April and October during Keeneland race meets. Children are allowed, but tours often include a description of how horses are bred. Comfortable clothes and sturdy shoes are highly recommended. Tipping the farm representative ($5–10) is customary, unless using a tour company that includes this.

Group or Private Guided
Blue Grass Tours (859) 252-5744
Horse Country (859) 963-1004, visithorsecountry.com

Group Guided
Horse Farm Tours, Inc. (859) 268-2906 or (800) 976-1034
Thoroughbred Heritage Horse Farm Tours (859) 260-8687
Unique Horse Farm Tours (859) 213-6653

Private Guided
Destination Bluegrass (859) 264-7822
Central Kentucky Tours (859) 492-3413
Horses of Kentucky: Lois Hill (859) 277-4625
Kentucky Horse Tours: Mary Ann Squires (859) 312-1124
Lexington in Touch, Inc. (859) 224-4226
Lexington Private Tours: John Midbo (859) 278-9488
Mint Julep Tours (502) 396-5682
Scott Goodlett Events (859) 361-3539
Prime Horse Tours (401) 699-4596
Thoroughbred Heritage Tours:
Larry and Linda Miano, (859) 260-8687
UnBridled Tours: Nancy Hapgood (859) 806-9688 or
Martha Martin (859) 333-8940

Self-Guided
VisitLex Lexington Walk and Bluegrass Country Driving Tour
visitlex.com/things-to-do/tours/

Individual farms by appointment
visitlex.com/idea-guide/horse-farm-tours/

STAY IN THE HEART OF DOWNTOWN
AT 21C MUSEUM HOTEL

Positioned in one of downtown Lexington's most prominent historic buildings, 21c Museum Hotel is so much more than a place to sleep. Cutting-edge art exhibits line the walls and fill the spaces of the first two floors while the scent of fine cuisine from the on-site, upscale Lockbox restaurant wafts throughout the space. Visitors take photos with larger-than-life-size blue penguins and enjoy upscale accommodations merely seconds from some of the city's trendiest bars and eateries. The guest rooms are decorated in a contemporary style with all the plush elegance of a boutique hotel. 21c is a place for the most fashionable visitor who wants unique and creative lodging amid an urban backdrop that features the best of the Bluegrass.

67 W. Main St., Lexington, KY 40507
(859) 899-6800, 21cmuseumhotels.com

FLY HIGH
AT THE AVIATION
MUSEUM OF KENTUCKY

The Aviation Museum of Kentucky proves there really is something for everyone in Lexington. Located at Bluegrass Airport, the dynamic space overflows with all things flight worthy ranging from a "Blue Angels" A-4 Skyhawk, a rare Crosley Moonbeam biplane, a Cessna 150, an interactive helicopter display, an F14, and loads of other colorful aircraft both suspended from the ceiling and displayed right on the floor where visitors can get an intimate look. Many of the planes are flyable, and the museum regularly hosts special events including opportunities to fly like Waldo Wright's Flying Service, where enthusiasts can ride with an experienced guide in a stock 1942 Boeing Stearman just as World War II pilots did. There's also a gift shop where even the youngest aspiring aeronaut can find a worthy souvenir of their visit.

4029 Airport Rd., Lexington, KY 40510
(859) 231-1219, museum@aviationky.org
aviationky.org

SEE A SHOW
AT THE LYRIC THEATRE &
CULTURAL ARTS CENTER

This building's beautifully restored façade stands as a testament to its historic significance in Lexington's downtown East End neighborhood. The original tile floors and box office were preserved and invite visitors into the more modernized and aesthetic space perfect for performances and events. The Lyric Theatre & Cultural Arts Center honors diversity and inclusivity, hosting everything from a Latin art exhibit to an old time radio hour featuring grassroots music to a women's art and writing workshop. Events change with the seasons as well, with series like Terror Tuesdays in October—a learning experience about African Americans in horror films. Neighbors and community members are encouraged to plan and attend events at The Lyric to enjoy both its history and its current place as a microcosm for Lexington as a whole.

300 E. Third St., Lexington, KY 40508
(859) 280-2218, lexingtonlyric.com

PLAN AN EVENT
AT THE BODLEY BULLOCK HOUSE

The Bodley Bullock House is best known as one of Lexington's most idyllic wedding venues, but its brilliant beauty should not be missed by history buffs. Many styles of architecture and furnishings are found in the home, including Victorian, Greek Revival, and Federal—perhaps most notably in its stunning three-story elliptical staircase. Each room is more lovely than the last, with gleaming wide-plank hardwood floors, timeless wallpaper patterns, and classic antique furniture pieces. Visitors can imagine a time gone by when ladies would float down the steps and out into the perennial garden to gossip over afternoon tea. Located in scenic Gratz Park, this stunning home is a perfect place to plan a wedding in downtown Lexington.

200 E. Market St., Lexington, KY 40508
(859) 252-8014, lexjrleague.com/?nd=bodley_bullock_house&und=150

TIP
The home is available for group tours by appointment or during events such as LexArts Hop and haunted tours.

DON'T COMPROMISE ON HISTORY
AT ASHLAND, THE HENRY CLAY ESTATE

The Henry Clay estate, named for the ash trees scattered around the grounds, is a sight to behold in one of Lexington's oldest and most picturesque neighborhoods. Stately and impressive, the large historic home sits on a twenty-acre lawn complete with gardens, walking paths, and various works of art. Visitors can tour the eighteen-room mansion furnished with period pieces and hear tales of yesteryear from knowledgeable docents or opt for an outdoor stroll through the arboretum on the Art & Grounds tour. There's even an offering focused on nine ladies connected to Ashland who helped change the world for women in the nineteenth and twentieth centuries. After all this walking and learning, folks can relax at the Ginkgo Tree Café in the yard and enjoy a light lunch offering of sandwiches, salads, soups, and desserts in the pristine surroundings.

120 Sycamore Rd., Lexington, KY 40502
(859) 266-8581, henryclay.org

TIP

The café is open Tuesday through Saturday from 9:00 to 3:00 and groups of seven or more require a reservation. Arrive ten minutes before tour time for tickets in person and check-in.

WITNESS INNOVATION
AT FOODCHAIN

FoodChain is aptly named because its indoor aquaponics system does just that: creates food through a chain of planned causes and effects. A tour of this innovative method of food production is as fascinating as it is overwhelming and inspiring. Visitors are guided into a greenhouse area where trays of leafy greens, herbs, and vegetables float atop long, narrow pools of water. As you walk by the vegetation, you might be offered a sample of peppery arugula, and you'll definitely end at a giant fish tank teeming with tilapia. The greens filter water for the fish and the fish waste becomes fertilizer for the plants, technically completing the chain. However, being located in the innovative Breadbox alongside a restaurant, FoodChain supplies Smithtown Seafood with tilapia so guests there can also learn firsthand about the benefits of urban indoor food production.

Breadbox
501 W. Sixth St. #105, Lexington, KY 40508
(859) 428-8380, foodchainlex.org

TOUR THE ECCENTRICITIES
OF THE HEADLEY-WHITNEY MUSEUM

The Headley-Whitney Museum lies at the end of a drive through picturesque Kentucky farmland and offers a glimpse into the eccentric life and creations of famed jewel artist George W. Headley III. There are three main attractions: the Jewel Room & Library, the Shell Grotto, and the Rose Garden, each appropriately named. The building itself was designed artistically and includes features like rosewood doors with brass finishings, Greek columns, English windows, and Georgian moldings. Headley's collection of bibelots (pronounced "bib-loh": a French term meaning small, ornate, decorative object of beauty) is on display, and his 1500-volume library is available for private tours. The Shell Grotto is a converted garage and is exactly what the name implies—it is overwhelmingly unique and almost humorous. The knockout pink and red rose garden is the most recent addition, but there is always a new exhibit on display, keeping this museum a dynamic place to visit time and time again.

4435 Old Frankfort Pike, Lexington, KY 40510
(859) 255-6653, headley-whitney.org

TAKE
A MURAL TOUR OR CHALLENGE

Lexington is renowned for its beautiful farmland, but a mural boom in the 2010s has enhanced the attractiveness of its buildings as well. Strolling through downtown is a great way to see many of these massive and often intricate displays, but VisitLex also offers a "mural challenge" for those who prefer a bit of curation and a potential prize with their paintings. Participants email photos of five murals to receive a free poster as commemoration of their Bluegrass art experience. Whether you choose to use the tour as an incentivized game or as a chance to play your very own docent, you'll be sure to enjoy the experience of works like the colorful Water Street take on Kentucky's favorite son, the two "pages" of the international storybook series by Herakut, or the massive I am MO in the Distillery District.

VisitLex
visitlex.com/things-to-do/murals, biglex@visitlex.com

TIP
Two other sources of mural information are prhbtn.com and the Fabulous in Fayette blog: fabulousinfayette.com/2018/04/30/street-art-murals-lexington-kentucky-volume-i/

SHOPPING AND FASHION

SCOUT FOR VINTAGE FINDS
AT SCOUT ANTIQUE AND MODERN

Carrie Bradshaw is quoted as saying, "When I first moved to New York and I was totally broke, sometimes I would buy *Vogue* instead of dinner. I felt it fed me more."

Similarly, a lunch break in Lexington is often better spent perusing Scout Antique & Modern than hitting the break room vending machines. It just feeds you more. The furniture ranges from classic antiques to mid-century modern, but the real treasures are the artistic creations and signature finds. Scout has a way of curating traditional history with retro charm into an experience more like a visit to an art museum than a day of antiquing. Whether you're in search of the perfect Louis Vuitton for date night or a *Mad Men*–style sofa, Scout is the place to find it.

935 Liberty Rd., Lexington, KY 40505
(859) 288-5200, scoutlexington.com

WINDOW SHOP
AT KEENELAND MERCANTILE

City Center in downtown Lexington may hold the record as Lexington's longest project, but its culmination in 2019 led to the opening of the elegant Keeneland Mercantile on Main Street. An extension of the storied and lovely boutique gift shop located at Keeneland's track on the outskirts of town, Keeneland Mercantile brings Kentucky goods closer to visitors and downtown dwellers alike. The light-filled, fresh venue displays locally sourced artisan crafts and products, all with horse history and legend in mind. From leather and silver goods to handblown glassware and bourbon-inspired foods to everything but the alcohol for a mint julep, Keeneland Mercantile offers the best of Bluegrass finery. On-site heat-stamping is also available for any items that could use a little personalization.

City Center
120 W. Main St., Lexington, KY 40507
(859) 288-4155, keenelandmercantile.com

GIGGLE
AT GEAR FROM
KENTUCKY FOR KENTUCKY

From gold-plated KFC chicken bone necklaces, to "the gift that's worse than nothing" boxes of Appalachian coal, this store has made an impact on our state's sense of humor. Shirts, socks, bourbon glasses and other gifts display hilarious KY themed images and wordplay perfect for souvenirs.

KY for KY has lots of tales to tell, but one favorite is of its mascot Cocaine Bear. The story goes that Bluegrass Conspiracy legend Andrew Thornton fell to his death pushing loads of cocaine out of a plane over the Chattahoochee Forest. Three months later, a black bear was found dead in the area and a necropsy revealed the cause as overdose. Someone brilliant had the foresight to taxidermy the bear and it ended up traveling the world—even being owned by Waylon Jennings at one point. When KY for KY found out, they tracked down "Pablo Escobear" and brought him home where he now teaches Kentucky children to stay off drugs.

kyforky.com

TIP
The Fun Mall location and NoLi district host a first Friday vendor fair called the Night Market from May to December. nolicdc.org/the-night-market

KY for KY Fun Mall
720 Bryan Ave., Lexington, KY 40505
(859) 303-6359

KY for KY Fun Stall
119 Marion, Suite 140, Lexington, KY 40517
(859) 687-1177

SHOP AND TALK
AT MULBERRY & LIME

Colorful mats strung between tree and house swing in the breeze and greet visitors to this gorgeous classic furnishing and gift shop. Mulberry & Lime is set in the historic Matthew Kennedy House on North Limestone in downtown Lexington. The spacious rooms with high ceilings overflow with the finest quality linens, toiletries, gifts, china, writing paper, accessories, and antiques, all curated by the owner who lived in the home as a child. Often featured on the LexArts Hop for its collection of local artwork, this is a great stop for a bite, shopping, or just a friendly chat with the knowledgeable and lover-of-all-things-Lexington proprietor. Mulberry & Lime has a wedding registry and offers unique gift wrap as well.

216 N. Limestone, Lexington, KY 40507
(859) 231-0800, mulberryandlime.com

AVOID BIG BOX STORES
AT POPS RESALE SHOP

Previously Owned Products, or POPS, is a place to find anything and everything you never knew you needed. The extensive collection of vinyl lining the skinny front corridor leads to a wide opening filled with vintage clothing, audio equipment, accessories, and kitsch of every shape and size. Lovers of all things retro can spend hours picking through the multitude of quirky items available for sale. The place is literally waiting for folks to record their own '80s montage of dress-up and photo ops with all the props it has to offer. POPS prides itself on being affordable, relevant, ever-changing, and a haven for the shopper who dreads big box and chain stores.

1423 Leestown Rd. B, Lexington, KY 40511
(859) 254-7677, popsresale.com

SMOKE A STOGIE
AT SCHWAB'S PIPES 'N' STUFF

When most people hear "Schwab's" they think of investing and retirement, but Lexingtonians know it's actually THE place to go for smoke aficionados. Schwab's Pipes 'n' Stuff was started in 1977 by a family who truly appreciated one of Kentucky's largest cash crops in the form of pipe smoking. The "'n' Stuff" was added to include their additional specialties in cigars and even premier shaving supplies. Anyone who appreciates the nostalgic smell of a pipe freshly tamped with tobacco will enjoy a visit to the shop. And if you're new to the smoking game, never fear! Jeff and Pat (lovingly known as "Mom") Schwab are certified tobacconists and will happily educate you on all the basics. In addition to shopping, they offer a patio with a fire pit and a smoking lounge with TV and wi-fi where shoppers can enjoy their purchases and perhaps take in an exciting UK game.

245 Southland Dr., Lexington, KY 40503
(859) 266-1011, schwabspipesnstuff.com

FIND
SOMETHING SPECIAL
AT SQECIAL MEDIA

Like something out of a John Hughes movie, Sqecial Media has been a campus anchor for over forty-five years. It might get categorized as a bookstore, but it really is so much more than the written word or even the items it has to sell. You can feel how special Sqecial is as soon as you enter. The associates are friendly and helpful, and the owner has been quoted as loving everything they sell, which includes coloring books, soaps, bumper stickers, salt and pepper shakers, and tarot cards, just to name a few. A visit to this magical place is more about the experience than the cash register, even if you do buy a bunch of funny magnets to take home to friends.

371 S. Limestone #220, Lexington, KY 40508
(859) 255-4316, sqecialmedia.tumblr.com

PICK UP A PRETTY PURSE
AT STREET SCENE

Street Scene is all things vintage. Covering decades from the 1950s all the way to the best parts of the '90s, Street Scene offers clothing and accessories along with furniture and home goods that all have the perfect "patina." Since 2007, the shop has overflowed with owner and consignment finds to thrill shoppers of all ages. It's a walk back in time where you might find your exact Smurfs lunchbox from fifth grade or the perfect pink jelly bracelets you used to hook together on your wrist. Whether you're looking to purchase a memento or just window shop for laughs, Street Scene has got you covered. But don't bother asking about the vintage blue fridge: it isn't for sale; it's more like the shop mascot. Which is kind of cooler.

2575 Regency Rd., Lexington, KY 40503
(859) 260-1578, streetscenevintage.com

BUY SOMETHING FUNKY
AT THE DOMESTIC

Part vintage home goods and clothing, part child of the '80s museum, the Domestic is always entertaining and often the only place to find that perfect eclectic piece. Need a set of Soviet leader nesting dolls? Have to have an antique hinged dental tooth model? Pining for a 1970s Elvis decanter? The Domestic is here to help! The whole shop is tirelessly curated to be an oasis of all things retro and mid-century so visitors can find just the right Coca-Cola t-shirt to go with their high-waisted, tapered leg Bugle Boys in one place. The location is somewhat off the beaten path, but the Domestic is a shining testament to just how quirky and wonderful a shopping district like the Warehouse Block can be.

945 National Ave., Lexington, KY 40502
(859) 309-3603, thedomesticlex.com

RELAX AND UNWIND WITH A GOOD FIND
AT WILD FIG BOOKS AND COFFEE

On a walk through the NoLi district, Wild Fig's beautifully converted old home stands out as one of the most welcoming structures on its street. Started by Kentucky writer Crystal Wilkinson and her partner Ronald Davis, the current location has added much to its neighborhood by providing a "sacred space" that invites everyone to come in, sit down, and enjoy some Smokin' Aces Coffee while perusing a delicious read. In addition to coffee and books, Wild Fig hosts some of the area's most unique and beloved events, such as drag queen story times and even small concerts. Wild Fig Books and Coffee is the only black-owned bookstore in Kentucky, and it's right here in Lexington for all to enjoy.

726 N. Limestone, Lexington, KY 40508
(859) 739-3207, wildfigbooksandcoffee.com

LOSE YOURSELF AMONG THE STACKS
AT JOSEPH BETH BOOKSELLERS

From the moment you enter under the famous green roof, you can tell that Jo-B is so much more than just books. Sunlight reflects off the lake and gleams in through the back windows of the impressive two-story space. The shop itself is like a choose-your-own-adventure book from childhood: a turn to the left will take you meandering through local and brand-name gifts and accessories until you ultimately arrive at Brontë Bistro for a light lunch or afternoon latte. A right turn takes you through aisles of books, games, music, and everything you expect a top bookseller to have. A straight-ahead walk leads you to the escalator where you feel like Kevin McAllister as you descend into children's heaven scattered with toys, clothing, science experiments, and all things geared to the young and young-at-heart. Joseph Beth is not only one of the best bookstores in town, it's a Lexington landmark.

161 Lexington Green Cir. B, Lexington, KY 40503
(859) 273-2911, josephbeth.com

SUPPORT LOCAL
AT A FARMERS MARKET

No matter what time, day, or part of town needed, Bluegrass farmers work hard to make fresh products available and accessible. In addition to the expected fruits and vegetables, area farmers markets offer live entertainment, crafts, artisan products, fresh flowers, meats, eggs, coffee, craft brews, local wine, and just about anything else to make a visit complete. Lexington Farmers Market is the longest running and is open throughout the year on every day except Monday and Friday. Bluegrass Farmers Market holds the distinction of being Kentucky Proud, meaning all items are grown in-state, and is held on Saturdays and most Tuesdays. Other events include the Evening Farmers Market, Lexington Makers Market, Chevy Chase Farmers Market, and the Cold Brew Coffee Festival.

TIP
Be sure to do an online search before attending any market, as weather and participation can affect availability.

Lexington Farmers Market
Tuesdays & Thursdays:
Maxwell St. & South Broadway parking lot
Wednesdays: The Summit at Fritz Farm
Saturdays:
Fifth Third Pavilion at Cheapside Park
251 W. Main St.
Sundays: 300 block of Southland Dr.
lexingtonfarmersmarket.com

Bluegrass Farmers Market
1837 Plaudit Pl., Lexington, Kentucky
(843) 325-7817, facebook.com/BluegrassFarmersMarket

Chevy Chase Farmers Market
200 Colony Blvd., Lexington, Kentucky 40502
farmersoncolony@gmail.com
facebook.com/Chevy-Chase-Farmers-Market-1601213506822092

DECORATE YOUR DREAM HOME
AT HOUSE BY JSD

Before anyone had heard of Chip and Joanna, Lexington had House. The culmination of the three owners' childhood dream, House by JSD is a flagship store in the Warehouse Block shopping district. One step into the meticulously designed space, and it is evident there is love behind every piece deemed worthy of inclusion in this esthetic. Inspired by the belief that the "unexpected and traditional can go hand in hand," tables filled with eclectic jewelry and elegant silk floral arrangements lead to chic linen chairs playfully accented with printed burlap throw pillows. In addition to enjoying this inspiring retail space, House clients can also take advantage of custom window treatments, reupholstery, and the expert designers who will do exactly what they're known for around here and "help your home tell your story."

1148 Industry Rd., Lexington, KY 40505
(859) 523-3933, housebyjsd.com

FIND SOME LUCK
AT FÁILTE IRISH IMPORTS

Fáilte (that's "welcome" in Gaelic) to the Lexington destination for heritage goods! For those who've ever seen the Emerald Isle, a drive through Central Kentucky horse country will quickly explain why so many Irish and Scottish settlers decided the Bluegrass should be their new home. This tiny shop tucked between a pub and a restaurant feels just right for its purpose of providing cherished pieces reminiscent of another land. Making the most of the space, rugby shirts and Hanna caps are piled on tables that also display Celtic jewelry, imported foods, Belleek china, Irish fragrances, and many more unique items. Also known as "The Irish Shop," a visit here is a must to complete any trip to Lexington.

113 S. Upper St., Lexington, KY 40507
(859) 381-1498, lexirish.com

TAKE THE BUTCHER'S WORD FOR IT
AT CRITCHFIELD MEATS

From an era when every customer was on a first name basis with their butcher, Critchfield Meats honors that tradition and is in its third generation of family ownership. Grandpa Amos, also known as "Butch" (short for butcher) established this local icon in 1969, and Lexingtonians have benefitted from the best quality meats ever since. The walls are lined with freezers of the finest Kentucky Proud products and the counter is staffed by the nicest and most knowledgeable butchers anywhere. In addition to meat, the shop has plenty of grocery options to round out an entire evening meal. Patrons can even enjoy weekly cookouts on Fridays, complete with bluegrass pickin' and a grill filled with ribeye, chicken, burgers, hot dogs, and much more.

Retail
2220 Nicholasville Rd., Ste 166, Lexington, KY 40503
(859) 276-4965

Wholesale
2285 Danforth Dr., Lexington, KY 40511
(859) 255-6021

critchfieldmeats.com

MEAT LOCALS
AT BLUEGRASS STOCKYARDS
REGIONAL MARKETPLACE

The original Bluegrass Stockyards tragically burned to the ground in 2016, but instead of "having a cow" about it, the resilient owners used the opportunity to create a revolutionary marketplace that serves as a resource not only for farmers, but also for the community as a whole. As extensive as it is unique, visitors can explore the space for hours of shopping, eating, and learning about the cattle industry in Kentucky. There's a state-of-the-art education center complete with an interactive eating cow, a museum showcasing artifacts and historic photographs, and several shops with farrier and breeder supplies, gifts, and apparel. A walk around the 232,000-square-foot facility is sure to work up an appetite, so folks can hit Hayden's Stockyard Eatery for some true Kentucky fare and sweet tea served with a side of southern hospitality.

4561 Iron Works Pike, Lexington, KY 40511
(859) 255-7701, bgregionalmarketplace.com

DRESS IN VINTAGE STYLE
AT THE BLACK MARKET

Located in one of Lexington's most recognizable and established shopping districts, the Black Market is a fantastic spot for the fashionable. Self-proclaimed as "vintage inspired," meaning "We love round-toed shoes and high-waisted skirts but like the fit of new," this boutique carries limited quantities to give every piece a unique feel. A poofy pendant hangs from the painted tile ceiling and sheds light while also mimicking the funky finds within the place. Wooden crates are stacked and mounted to provide shelving for sterling silver jewelry and other accessories, colorful pumps are displayed on an antique sewing machine, and ornate mirrors litter the walls further enhancing the distinctive atmosphere. Whether you need a new dress for date night or just the right accessory for every day, the Black Market is sure to please.

516 E. High St., Lexington, KY 40502
(859) 281-1421, theblackmarketboutique.com

APPRECIATE CREATIVITY
AT ARTIQUE GALLERY

Artique is truly a place to get lost and treat your senses for a few hours. Imagine colorful hand-blown glass dangling from the ceiling, reflecting brilliant light on displays of sculpted aluminum yard art and carved wooden wall hangings. There are glass cases overflowing with teardrop gem earrings, sterling silver pendant necklaces, copper wrist cuffs, and striking rings of all shapes and sizes. Shelves and tables hold locally crafted soaps and toiletries along with plush, warm scarves and unique artisan kitchen goods like wooden bowls and pasta forks. The friendly employees act as docents in this museum-turned-retail shop. You're bound to find the perfect gift for that special someone, even if that someone is you.

Fayette Mall
3555 Nicholasville Rd., #921, Lexington, KY 40503
(859) 272-8802, artiquegallery.com

TASTE A BOURBON CHERRY
AT OLD KENTUCKY CHOCOLATES

Old Kentucky Chocolates has been crafting with Lexington pride since 1964, but don't let the name fool you—they offer so much more than their signature bourbon balls and cherries made exclusively with 100-proof Jim Beam. The smell of chocolate tickles your nose while you browse the vast selection of cocoa-covered delicacies and assorted sweet treats, and the tables overflowing with UK apparel, decorative home goods, and local artisan crafts call to you as mementos of your time in this Central Kentucky landmark. Anyone throwing a Derby party, or just looking for a great souvenir, knows not to miss OKC. People in the Bluegrass love Old Kentucky Chocolates so much that it has expanded to three locations, so there's always a place nearby to get your fix.

450 Southland Dr., Lexington, KY
(859) 278-4444

Hamburg Shopping Center, 1890 Star Shoot Pkwy., Lexington, KY
(859) 554-0988

Lansdowne Shoppes, 3385 Tates Creek Rd., Lexington, KY
(859) 268-4711, oldkycandy.com

CUSTOMIZE A PRESENT
AT PEGGY'S GIFTS & ACCESSORIES

In Lexington, a present wrapped in pink and white polka dot paper lets the receiver know they're special because someone took the time to hit Peggy's Gifts & Accessories. Located on Clay Avenue and named for its owner, this cozy store is an old home converted to girly shopping heaven. Room after room overflows with the most squeal-worthy and precious gifts, from totes and purses to jewelry and home accessories. Staff are warm, engaging, and helpful, and they work hard to make life easier by offering personalization on almost any item along with their signature gift wrap. Peggy's appeals to clients of all ages by including specific offerings like gifts exclusively for sororities, UK fans, and infants.

112 Clay Ave., Lexington, KY 40502
(859) 255-3188, peggysgifts.com

SUGGESTED ITINERARIES

VINTAGE AND RETRO

Scout for Vintage Finds at Scout Antique and Modern, 110

Plan a Date Night at Carson's Food and Drink, 11

Watch a Movie at the Kentucky Theater, 53

Drive in to the Parkette, 27

Pick Up a Pretty Purse at Street Scene, 118

Grab Breakfast at Wheeler Pharmacy, 20

Dress in Vintage Style at the Black Market, 128

DOWNTOWN TIME

Stay in the He*art* of Downtown at 21c Museum Hotel, 98

Try the Tapas at Corto Lima, 14

Take a Taste-Bud Tour with Brunch in the Bluegrass, 17

Get a History Lesson at Visit Lex, 86

Take a Mural Tour or Challenge, 106

Find Some First Lady Insight at the Mary Todd Lincoln House, 92

Pay It Forward at a Cup of Commonwealth, 24

• •

DRINK TIME

GIRL TIME

PLAY TIME

KID TIME

Stop Adulting for a Day at Explorium, 50

Savor Explosively Good Ice Cream at Crank & Boom, 2

Stroll Through the Arboretum, 58

Say Your Prayers at Lexington Ice Center Mini Golf, 70

Do-Nut Miss Breakfast at Spalding's Bakery, 8

EQUINE EVERYTHING

Tailgate at Keeneland, 72

Trot On Over to the Kentucky Horse Park, 67

Experience Local at a Ouita Restaurant, 18

Bet On the Ponies at the Red Mile, 82

Window Shop at Keeneland Mercantile, 111

ACTIVITIES BY SEASON

SPRING

SUMMER

FALL

WINTER

INDEX

● ●